— WHY —
CHRISTIANS
MUST BE RIGHT

BRAHM FRENCH

WestBow
PRESS
A DIVISION OF THOMAS NELSON

Scripture taken from the King James Version of the Bible.

WestBow Press books may be ordered through booksellers or by contacting:

WestBow Press
A Division of Thomas Nelson
1663 Liberty Drive
Bloomington, IN 47403
www.westbowpress.com
1-(866) 928-1240

ISBN: 978-1-4497-4633-9 (sc)
ISBN: 978-1-4497-4634-6 (e)

Library of Congress Control Number: 2012906300

Printed in the United States of America

WestBow Press rev. date: 04/17/2012

For
Alana
Brianna
Chandler (Chaney)
And all who love liberty

I would like to thank my family for allowing
me the time to write without
much complaint.

A huge Thank You goes to Kelly Follis
and family for the time and energy that it
took to invest in this book.

CONTENTS

PREFACE

Late February, the wind blowing at my back as I waited on my neighbor, I stood on the porch and looked at the decorations that lined the yard and the entrance to the home. A wooden Americana Yankee Doodle Dandy hung on the exterior wall alongside another wooden Americana flag. On the other side of the porch were more reminders of this great land.

Thoughts of my childhood and the Great Nation that was handed to me flooded my mind. I recounted in my thoughts the freedoms that were passed down from previous generations. My chest swelled with pride, I had the opportunity to be an American from birth.

That emotion consumed me for a brief moment, until I began to think of my children and the America that they are receiving from us. With this realization, my eyes began to mist, and I began to make a silent prayer for this nation. The America our children are experiencing is not the same America we grew up enjoying. Oh the flag still has thirteen stripes and it still has white stars against a dark blue velvet backdrop, but the meaning to some is something completely different today.

America was a place where hope sprung forth from a foundation of personal liberty. A liberty that said you can be what you want, if you are willing to work long and hard enough to do it. Today, many voices in America are using the same phrases, but mean things entirely different. The hope that sprung forth, they now say is in government. The liberty they speak of is not from government intrusion, but liberty to get whatever you want from government. True personal liberty has, for the most part, been thrown into the ash heap of history in the minds of many.

This simply will not do. America holds too much potential for us to let her slip away. We owe our children more than a symbol of what America used to be or stories of what it was like to be free. I pray our children will sing the words, "land of the free and home of the brave" with more than feeling, with meaning.

There has come a vacuum in the land. This vacuum has tried to eradicate God from the hearts and minds of the people. We have been told that the void that remains should be filled by government.

The future of this nation rests in the hands of what seems to be a reluctant people, a people that are told to remain silent, that are told they are the minority, a people who are ridiculed in the public square. These are the ones for whom this book is written. The apostle Paul wrote to Timothy and instructed him to, "Stir up the gift of God, which is in thee . . . For God hath not given us the spirit of fear; but of power, and of love, and of a sound mind. Be not thou therefore ashamed of the testimony of our Lord . . ." (2 Timothy 1:6-8)

CHAPTER 1

GROUP THINK/
POLITICAL CORRECTNESS

Two men have just been arrested after being used by God to perform a miracle. The reason for the arrest: declaring that the miracle was performed through the power of the name of Jesus Christ. The court's ruling was probation on one condition: that they speak no more in the name of Jesus. In other words, "We will let you go if you just shut up and sit down." The men's response was loud and clear, "Whether it be right in the sight of God to hearken unto you more than unto God, judge ye." Eventually one of these men was crucified upside down and the other was put live in boiling oil and banished to a deserted island all because they would not give in to the political correctness of the hour. Let's back up and examine this a little further. (Paraphrased from Acts chapters 3 and 4)

Jesus has just been crucified, raised from the dead, ascended into heaven, and the Holy Ghost has just been poured out. Peter stands up with the other disciples and delivers a convicting message. In this message he tells those gathered there that this Jesus that they just crucified is the

Christ. He also makes some astonishing claims that I believe will help us as Christians. He says:

> Act 2:22-23 Ye men of Israel, hear these words; Jesus of Nazareth, a man approved of God among you by miracles and wonders and signs, which God did by him in the midst of you, as ye yourselves also know: 23) Him, being delivered by the determinate counsel and foreknowledge of God, ye have taken, and by wicked hands have crucified and slain:

I am so grateful that He shed His perfect pure blood for you and me. Without the shedding of blood there is no remission of sins. However, I would like to look at the other parties involved. He places the blame of the crucifixion of the Lord at the feet of the "determinate counsel and foreknowledge of God." Peter continues:

> Act 2:40 And with many other words did he testify and exhort, saying, Save yourselves from this untoward generation.

Save yourselves from this . . . generation, a generation that blindly followed the determinate counsel. Peter is speaking to those who have gathered in Jerusalem, the same city outside of which Jesus was crucified. It was these same people who had cried out for His crucifixion. Peter declares that they are untoward. In other words, they are warped, perverse, and crooked. To have a better understanding of what happened, Matthew gives his account:

> Matthew 26:59-66 Now the chief priests, and elders, and all the council, sought false witness against Jesus, to put

him to death;60) But found none: yea, though many false witnesses came, yet found they none. At the last came two false witnesses,61) And said, This fellow said, I am able to destroy the temple of God, and to build it in three days.62) And the high priest arose, and said unto him, Answerest thou nothing? what is it which these witness against thee?63) But Jesus held his peace. And the high priest answered and said unto him, I adjure thee by the living God, that thou tell us whether thou be the Christ, the Son of God.64) Jesus saith unto him, Thou hast said: nevertheless I say unto you, Hereafter shall ye see the Son of man sitting on the right hand of power, and coming in the clouds of heaven.65) Then the high priest rent his clothes, saying, He hath spoken blasphemy; what further need have we of witnesses? behold, now ye have heard his blasphemy.66) What think ye? They answered and said, He is guilty of death.

It was the chief priests, elders, and all the council that urged the crowd forward. This does not excuse each individual, but it does give us a clearer understanding of what really transpired. In verse 1 of chapter 27 Matthew writes:

Matthew 27:1 When the morning was come, all the chief priests and elders of the people took counsel against Jesus to put him to death:

It was the leadership that took council against Him to put Jesus to death. Matthew continues:

Matthew 27:11-23 And Jesus stood before the governor: and the governor asked him, saying, Art thou the King of the Jews? And Jesus said unto him, Thou sayest.12) And when he was accused of the chief priests and elders, he answered nothing.13) Then said Pilate unto him, Hearest thou not how many things they witness against thee?14) And he answered him to never a word; insomuch that the governor marvelled greatly.15) Now at that feast the governor was wont to release unto the people a prisoner, whom they would.16) And they had then a notable prisoner, called Barabbas.17) Therefore when they were gathered together, Pilate said unto them, Whom will ye that I release unto you? Barabbas, or Jesus which is called Christ?18) For he knew that for envy they had delivered him.19) When he was set down on the judgment seat, his wife sent unto him, saying, Have thou nothing to do with that just man: for I have suffered many things this day in a dream because of him.20) But the chief priests and elders persuaded the multitude that they should ask Barabbas, and destroy Jesus.21) The governor answered and said unto them, Whether of the twain will ye that I release unto you? They said, Barabbas.22) Pilate saith unto them, What shall I do then with Jesus which is called Christ? They all say unto him, Let him be crucified.23) And the governor said, Why, what evil hath he done? But they cried out the more, saying, Let him be crucified.

Pilate followed the desires of the crowd. This is why I do not believe that we can lay all the blame at the feet of our politicians. They are only doing what we sent them to do. Verse 20 says that the "chief priests and elders persuaded the multitude". What we need is men, women, and children to think outside the box and inside the Book. People who choose to do what is right, not what is popular. Citizens who say what is right, not what is least likely to upset people.

It was political correctness and groupthink that led to the crucifixion of the Lord. This is not the only time masses of people acted out and did horrendous things to others because of blind obedience. In Nazi Germany, over 6 million Jews were killed due, in a large part, to group thought.

Political correctness has become expected in popular culture, but it has the exact same effect as the groupthink that crucified Jesus. It minimizes individual thought in order to maximize collective thought. History gives account after account of groupthink. It was groupthink that built the tower of Babel. Groupthink murmured and complained about Moses. Groupthink rejected Caleb and Joshua's faith that they could be victorious. It was groupthink that forced them into the wilderness for 40 years and kept them out of the land that the Lord had promised.

Personally, I have been silent far too long. Though I have paid attention to the things going on around me, I have said nothing. For the most part, even in the church that I pastor, I have kept silent about politics, thinking that politics does not belong in the Church. I was wrong. No longer can I be silent. You may not agree with me on all the issues that we will discuss, but I encourage you to stand against the tide of political correctness. We do not have to see eye to eye on every issue, but our country does need men, women, and even children who are willing to stand against the onslaught of propaganda and declare with a loud clear voice the truth of God's Word.

CHAPTER 2

PERSONAL CHOICE/
RESPONSIBILITY

One of the greatest tricks of groupthink and political correctness is to change the meaning of words. Drunk driving is now drinking and driving, alcoholism is now a disease, stealing is an impulse disorder, etc. By changing the words, the liberal elite have framed the argument to fit the picture they would like to paint. After the words have been changed to better suit their feelings, they begin to use those words to explain why those of us that hold to basic biblical principles are in error. Then the tables are turned and the predator is now the victim and vice versa.

This is in complete opposition to God and His Word. When the serpent in the garden beguiled Eve and she and Adam ate of the tree, they tried to pass the buck. Adam blamed Eve, Eve blamed the serpent. However, God held each one of them accountable for their own personal actions. (Genesis 3:1-19)

The politically correct movement would blame God for putting the tree in the garden in the first place. Today, we are told that the criminal is really the victim. An example of this thought process can be illustrated as follows: a woman leaves her purse in the car and a thug reaches through the open window and steals the purse. The woman is blamed because she left the purse in the car. The blame is greater if she left it in plain view, not to mention leaving the window open and the car unlocked. That poor thug had no choice but to take the purse.

So now the woman is put on the hot seat while the thug moves on to the next victim. This thought process is not in accordance with God's law, nor do I believe it is how He intended for society to operate. From the very beginning, there were consequences that followed actions. Eve was cursed with pain in child birth, Adam was cursed with having to live by the sweat of his brow (both were cursed with death) and the serpent was cursed by slithering on his belly.

Some now would blame God, saying things like, "I can't believe God would do that to them. I thought He was a God of love." Now God becomes the guilty party and not Adam and Eve. God ordained for man to have a free will. His desire was for them to serve Him; however, He knew that forced love is really no love at all. So, in His infinite wisdom, He left man an out.

Let's look at the story of the Garden of Eden through a different lens. If today's political establishment was to play the role of God in the garden, (a dream come true for most of them) a significant schism would be apparent among those in power. The knee—jerk reaction from some among the ruling class would be to chop down the Tree of Knowledge of Good and Evil, in order to stop the possibility that someone might eat from it. But the other faction would want to tax all those who ate the forbidden fruit. This theory of taxation is known as "sin tax."

Both factions would be in error and would create unintended ramifications. If the tree were cut down by the government, people would not have the opportunity to decide to do what is right. The only situation in which we can make a decision to do what is right is when we are faced with choosing between right and wrong. Only then are we able to reject the wrong and choose correctly.

The problem with a "sin tax" is that while it discourages the actions of society, government grows accustomed to the income generated by that action. Therefore; government wants no deliverance from the sin, due to the possibility of lost revenue. Rather, government would want more people to eat of the tree.

Is it wrong to eat of the tree? Yes. However, it is a choice that each individual will have to make for themselves. Government has no place in the discussion. Laws are passed by government to either encourage or discourage our behavior.

Most laws that discourage our negative behavior towards others, such as stealing, rape, or murder are good laws and are appropriate in governing society. However, laws that are imposed on us for our own safety, security, or any other reason are bad laws. For instance, it is against the law for me to come into your house and steal your computer; that is a good law. But a law against me using my own computer in my own home that I purchased with my own money would be a bad law.

Some laws that constrain one's negative actions against another person fail to measure up to the standards of the principle of creation. For instance, if you own a restaurant in which you allow smoking and I am a non-smoker with asthma who enters your establishment, the law could say that the smoke had a negative impact on me. This would be a bad law. The principle of creation would say that I could leave your establishment. That would be my personal choice and responsibility.

Though, I do not smoke and hope my children never smoke, my logic is entirely different than the logic of those who would use government to limit the liberties of others. I do not smoke because my body is the temple of the Holy Ghost; this is also why I hope my children would not smoke. True freedom only comes with the right to make the wrong choice.

Laws were established for your safety, not from you, but from me, and vice versa. If the law tries to protect you from you, it is bad; however, if the law protects you from another, it is good. Every law that infringes on the rights of others or puts the rights of one above another is strictly contrary to the principles of creation.

Isn't it amazing that God only had one law in the garden. That tells me there is no utopia on earth. The closest we will ever see of a utopia is in the face of a free and liberated people. In the Garden there was only one law, Moses went up onto the mount and came back with ten, however, by the end of the Old Testament there were six hundred and thirteen laws. More laws did not bring God's people closer to Him, but were a sign that they were drifting further away from Him. We do not need more laws, we need more God.

If as a society, we walked closer to Him; we would rely more on Him and less on the government for our answers. Those in power recognize this fact and realize that God must be systematically removed from society in order to maintain their power. The void that is left by the absence of God is filled by the State. As Christians, our desire is to have more of Him and more of God means less government.

CHAPTER 3

LIMITED GOVERNMENT

During the time God was establishing Israel, as recorded in the Bible in the book of Leviticus, He gave His people the model for charitable behavior. Government played no part in it. When the farmer reaped the harvest, he was to leave the corners of the field un-harvested and he was not to gather the gleanings. He was to leave part of his harvest for the poor and the stranger. (Leviticus 19:9-11). It was never God's will for the government to provide for those in need. Instead, He meant for the individual to provide for his home and his neighbor who was unable to care for himself.

This same principle is found in Deuteronomy. If a sheaf was forgotten in the field, it was to be left there for the stranger, the fatherless, and the widow. As a matter of fact, God declared that He would bless the work of the hands that left the sheaf for another. The Lord then reminded Israel that they were bondmen (slaves) in the land of Egypt and instructed them not to forget the condition from which He rescued them. In other words, the Lord was saying, "don't forget where you came from or where I found you." (Deuteronomy 24:19-22)

The Bible is so clear that charity is required of God's people, it may seem reasonable for government to administer charitable giving. However, there are several reasons this is not a good idea. One of the reasons is that government is less efficient than individuals. Here is an illustration of this fact:

Let's say I walk past your apple orchard, and because I am hungry, I pick and eat ten apples. God's Word blesses this type of "charity." Now let us say that I am hungry and instead of exerting the energy it would take to pick the apples from your tree, I hire someone else to do it. Now we have a dilemma which is contrary to God's plan for charity. The problem comes because I have to pay the man who took the apples for me. If he takes the same ten apples but keeps some for himself (let's say four) I remain hungry because I only received six apples instead of the ten I needed to be full. God did not want those in need to go unfed so His plan is broken. And if the man takes more than the ten apples needed to satiate my hunger, he has stolen from you and broken God's law. In this scenario, the government plays the part of the hired middle man. Inevitably, he (government) takes twelve apples instead of the necessary ten, thereby stealing from you, the farmer. The government then gives me six apples, which leaves me hungry and lines its own pockets with the fruit of your labors.

This is precisely why government benefits from involvement in every aspect of our lives. The more it is involved, the more control, the more money, the more freedom it takes. The same principles that were found in the Old Testament are in the New Testament.

When the Church was established in Acts, the Bible said the new Christian, "Sold their possessions and goods, and parted them to all men, as every man had need." (Acts

2:42-47) This was not forced upon them; it was out of their hearts that they gave. Let me point out that this was done by the Church not by the government. A government big enough to give you what you want is big enough to take what you have.

The Apostle Paul gives a firsthand account of a lesson the government should learn. He writes, "Not that I speak in respect of want: for I have learned, in whatsoever state I am, therewith to be content. I know both how to be abased, and I know how to abound: everywhere and in all things I am instructed both to be full and to be hungry, both to abound and to suffer need. I can do all things through Christ which strengtheneth me." (Philippians 4:11-13)

Paul speaks of knowing how to abound and how to be abased. There is no question the federal government knows how to abound (at our expense). Wouldn't it be prudent for government to learn how to be abased? This lesson must be learned in our own lives. When money is short one month, what do you do? You probably cut back on the amount of money you spend, so you can be sure you have enough to pay your bills. Government does not know how to cut back. Politicians only know how to raise more taxes.

Try this the next time you have a month, when your expenses exceed your income: Walk into your boss' office and demand more money. Explain that if he does not give you the additional funds, he will lose some fundamental services that you provide. If he says no, then begin to threaten to take him to court and start looking for ways to have him put in jail. You may find yourself out of work and in the mental institution. However, this is exactly what the federal and even some state-level governments have done.

Every time the government grows, our liberties shrink. In recent times, our freedoms have further eroded with every passing day as government expands into more areas of our lives. Government has found its way into our jobs, cars, homes, and even bathrooms. We are required by law to wear seatbelts and our cars are legally limited to using only a certain amount of gas per mile etc. Regulators have told us we must use florescent light bulbs in our homes and have outlawed incandescent bulbs. Government agencies are now requiring us to pack "better" lunches for our children when they go to public school. Government has even entered our bathrooms and told us we use too much water (water that we pay for) when we flush our toilets. Government has regulated electric companies until they are forced out of business. Then the regulators tell us we are using too much energy and we need to cut back. Government forced banks to loan money to people who could never repay the funds and then blamed the banks for giving the loans. The government even required some unwilling banks to take federal funds as part of the much-publicized bank bail-out program. Why? Dependence produced by government money leads to increased government power.

Politicians who do not want to take the criticism for their poor decisions are able to hide behind unelected "officials" who work for government agencies that have the ability to raise taxes through fees and penalties, as well as harass the average citizen with excess regulation. Does the phrase "taxation without representation" sound familiar? This practice, which was one reason for the American Revolution, is once again prevalent in our country. When will it become too much for us? Are we the frog that is placed in the cool water on the stove? If so, the water will slowly get warmer before it boils us alive. Every day the flames under that pot are turned up. Who will speak up? Will any of us have the courage to jump out of the pot?

It is time to put the government on a crash diet. Not just the federal, but the state and local governments as well. As far as I know, I am the only one that sees some great things going on in this recent recession. The local news stations have been complaining about cities that have had to reduce their payrolls and layoff some of the "public servants" they employ. In my opinion, this is fantastic news. What, you ask? How can this be great news? People are losing their jobs and some of them are police officers and firefighters.

For now, I will use police officers, to explain why this is actually a good thing. I begin with this example because when police forces downsize, people become outraged. But here is how I look at it: if more police officers lose their jobs that means there is less useless work for those who are still employed. For instance, the cop that still has his job will be busy checking out the home that was just robbed rather than giving me a ticket for not wearing my seatbelt or because the light over my license plate has burned out.

It is time to remind the government officials that they work for us, not the other way around. Politicians and bureaucrats have forgotten they are the employees of the people. They go to Washington D.C., to our State Capitols, and to our hometown city halls to work for us. We do not go to our jobs to work for them.

It is time for our voices to be heard once again. Our taxes are too high, government regulations are strangling our productivity, and government has reached too far into our lives and the lives of our children.

CHAPTER 4

TAXES

Historically speaking, taxation was a key motivator for the American colonists to cut the umbilical cord with England. However, England was not the first nation in history to be divided over taxation without representation. In the Bible, 1 Kings gives some great insight into the harmful effects of over—taxation.

Upon the death of King Solomon, his son Rehoboam, rose to the throne and was made king. Jeroboam, who previously fled from King Solomon into Egypt, heard that the King had died. Upon receiving this news, Jeroboam returned to Israel and with the congregation of Israel spoke to Rehoboam. They told the new king, "Thy father made our yoke grievous: now therefore make thou the grievous service of thy father, and his heavy yoke which he put upon us, lighter, and we will serve thee."

Rehoboam asked Jeroboam and the people of Israel to leave for three days, and promised an answer upon their return. While Israel was gone, the king sought counsel. First, he went to the old men that had counseled his father. The advice they gave him was tremendous, "If thou wilt be a servant unto this people this day and wilt serve them, and answer them, and speak good words to them, then they will be thy servants for—ever."

However, the king forsook the counsel of the old men, and consulted with the young men with whom he had grown up. Their advice was the exact opposite of what the old men had advised. "Thus shalt thou speak unto this people that spoke to you, saying 'thy father made our yoke heavy, but make thou it lighter unto us;' thus shalt thou say unto them, 'my little finger shall be thicker than my father's loins. And now whereas my father did lade you with a heavy yoke, I will add to your yoke: my father hath chastised you with whips, but I will chastise you with scorpions.'"

Jeroboam and the people came back to Rehoboam on the third day as he had asked. His answer to them was, "My father made your yoke heavy, and I will add to your yoke: my father also chastised you with whips, but I will chastise you with scorpions."

When the people of Israel saw that the king had not listened to them, they were angry. The people realized their new king, whose lineage was through their beloved King David, had no concern for them and they wanted no part of Rehoboam's authority. They became enraged, and went to their tents to wait for the opportunity to be heard.

The time for them to make their opinions heard came when Rehoboam sent out Adoram, the tax collector. All of Israel stoned him to death. Israel rebelled against the house of David and Rehoboam in particular. The only tribe that followed the house of David was the tribe of Judah and a portion of the tribe of Benjamin. The rest of Israel made Jeroboam their king. (1 Kings 12:1-21)

I do not suggest that we kill the IRS man (1Kings 12:18), however, there are some solid principles that we can take from this story.

One of the quickest ways to divide a nation is to raise taxes beyond the bearable limits of those paying them. This will cause either a mass exodus of the people who are paying the taxes or will eventually lead to an uprising among the people with the goal being to dethrone the sitting "king."

If there is a mass exodus and the rich leave our country, who will hire those of us who have yet to acquire our wealth? Furthermore, what motivation would we have to seek greater wealth anyway? The reward for accumulating wealth is that the government will confiscate it. That type of policy does not induce productive behavior.

The only other option is to dethrone the "king." In America, of course we have no king, but we do have three houses that from time to time need to be cleaned: the Senate, the House of Representatives, and the White House. The time has now come to clean our houses. Currently many of the inhabitants of the houses are not governing in accordance with the will of the people and they are ruling without fear of retribution on Election Day. This attitude can only lead to increasing taxation and government regulation. Our America will sink into poverty because the rich will vacate the premises and take our chances of employment with them.

Taxes have an unseen effect on businesses, their owners, and those whom they employ. For example, several years ago, I owned a small business selling shoes. The business began to grow and before long it was doing quite well. I hired several employees and decided it was time to incorporate the business. Though I didn't have stockholders, I did have a boss outside my own company: the State.

One of the issues I faced was that as a retailer I was required to pay sales tax. This meant that some of the money I collected selling shoes had to be paid to the State. I could set the price of the product to include the tax payment, I could take taxes from my profits or I could determine that the business could not afford to operate with the additional cost of these taxes and close shop. I believed the best option for me was to include the sales tax in the price of the product and set the price at $12 per pair.

Being new to the world of business, I hadn't realized I needed to collect sales tax in the beginning. Prior to this discovery, I sold the shoes for $10 per pair. When the price was $10, I sold about 500 pairs in an average weekend. I purchased the shoes for $5 which would have resulted in a profit of $2,500. However, there were other expenses involved. The city where I sold the shoes was about two and a half hours from my home, so I commuted and stayed overnight at a motel. The cost of the motel room was at least $50 per night. I also rented the property where I was selling the shoes. That was $100. Fuel for the commute added another $160 to the cost, not to mention wear and tear on the vehicle. So my profit of $2,500 was reduced to 2,190. Furthermore, I had a partner with whom I split the profits making my net profit $1,095. Not bad for a weekend you may say.

However, when I realized I had to collect and pay sales tax and raised the price of a pair of shoes from $10 to $12, the average weekend sales dropped from 500 pairs to approximately 300 pairs. Unfortunately, none of our expenses decreased. Our only change was a lower profit margin. My net profit went from $1,095 to $595 in a weekend.

The people who were willing to buy 10 pairs of shoes for $100 were much less willing to buy 10 pairs for $120. Instead, they would buy less, and we would make less.

Eventually we closed shop. This means that our employees lost their jobs and had to look somewhere else for the funds they made from the business. It also means that the government no longer receives sales and income tax revenue from our operations. In other words, I no longer confiscate people's funds for them.

In the Bible, Luke tells the story of the birth of the Savoir. Let's let it speak for itself:

> Luke 2:1-7 And it came to pass in those days, that there went out a decree from Caesar Augustus, that all the world should be taxed. 2) (And this taxing was first made when Cyrenius was governor of Syria.) 3) And all went to be taxed, every one into his own city. 4) And Joseph also went up from Galilee, out of the city of Nazareth, into Judaea, unto the city of David, which is called Bethlehem; (because he was of the house and lineage of David: 5) To be taxed with Mary his espoused wife, being great with child. 6) And so it was, that, while they were there, the days were accomplished that she should be delivered. 7) And she brought forth her firstborn son, and wrapped him in swaddling clothes, and laid him in a manger; because there was no room for them in the inn.

Don't kid yourself; taxation still leaves mothers and children out in the cold of night. The Left has used class envy to pit the poor against the rich in order to raise taxes on the rich. However, the "good intentions" of the Left, never seem to work the way they are supposed to.

Do you think the rich men that went to Bethlehem to pay their taxes slept in the cold that night? No, they had servants that they most likely sent ahead, in order to secure a room for them; knowing that there would be huge crowds on their "April 15th" (tax day). The only ones left in the cold were the middle class, poor, and less fortunate.

Higher taxes do not bring wealth, but poverty. If you raise the taxes on the local convenience store to make that company pay its fair share; the store will raise its prices, try to cut back in other areas (such as reducing the hours of employees) or close its doors.

The prophet Daniel gives a prophecy of one who raises taxes. He writes, "Then shall stand up in his estate a raiser of taxes in the glory of the kingdom: but within few days he shall be destroyed, neither in anger, nor in battle." (Daniel 11:20)

What would remove this ruler? Please, Lord, please let it be an election. (Can you hear the inflection in my voice?)

We have lived to see a day when it appears that the predominant thought in our culture is that it is the government's job to feed, clothe, provide medical treatment, and generally care for the country's citizens from cradle to grave. God and His followers used to be the ones our countrymen turned to in times of need. I believe they still should.

When Jesus was asked by the Pharisees and the Herodians if it was lawful to pay taxes to Caesar, He responded, "Why tempt ye me? Bring me a penny, that I may see it . . . Whose is this image and superscription?" After they said that it was Caesar's, Jesus said, "Render to Caesar the things that are Caesar's, and to God the things that are God's." (Mark 12:13-17)

Here Jesus makes a clear distinction (to the chagrin of many in the welfare state of mind) between Government and the Church. However, as Government grows; the Church generally shrinks. Consider the food stamp program. If your family was in need of food, you used to be able to go to your church and your fellow members would disperse food to you as you needed it. However, now there is no need for the

Church (in the minds of many) to give out food. You can simply go down to your local Health and Human Services Department and they will give you food stamps or a card that can be used to purchase food at your local grocery store.

The Left does not really want separation of Church and State; they want a knitting of Church and State. In other words, they want them knit so closely together that to have one i.e. Church, you must worship at the altar of the other i.e. State. However, Jesus draws the line in Mark 12 "Render to Caesar the things that are Caesar's, and to God the things that are God's."

Now, the "Christian" Left (if there is such a thing) has a problem. So, they then must blur the lines that Jesus so clearly marked out. How do they do it? They take ministry from the Church and place it in the government. Therefore, we now have a government in facets of our lives that were meant to only be filled by God and the Church. This plays out in the streets, homes, schools, and on the jobs of many Americans today.

We have a population that fears the government but not the Creator. We can see this with the rise of sin and carnality; we panic when we see a police officer, when our taxes are due, or when we get a call or visit from some government official. But we don't think twice about missing church or skipping our personal prayer time.

We have been lied to and robbed by the government. Government and politicians have told us that they can meet all our needs, but the more they try to meet them, the more needs arise. It becomes a cycle. The more we yearn for freedom the tighter the strangle hold becomes. It is time for us as Christian Americans to stand up to the giant and demand that he get out of our lives and out of our pocket books.

CHAPTER 5

WELFARE STATE

Some of us have not been giving; we have been taking. But taking at what expense? Not at what expense to the government, but what expense to us and our neighbors? Whether it is a disability check that keeps us from seeking employment, or earned income tax credits (which can result in a payment from the IRS even if no income tax was paid to the IRS) or food stamps, or any of the thousand and one ways we get other people's money without doing any work. The actual victim becomes those of us who have grown accustomed to receiving something for nothing.

The disability check might sound good, until you realize you are not allowed to work, even if the work is something you are physically able to do. You have now sold yourself short and settled for less than what you could have achieved and earned. You may have settled for far less than what God might have had in mind for you. The same becomes true with food stamps, SSI, and other unearned entitlements.

Here is a personal story that might help make clear the defects of the welfare state:

Several years ago, I owned a small business. The business was doing moderately well. One year the federal government gave us money through a "tax credit" called the Child Tax Credit. We invested this money into the business. This was not money we had paid to the IRS. It had been paid to them by our fellow citizens.

When tax time came around the next year; we expected to get money back again. However, when we filled out our return and reported how we had used the tax credit from the previous year, we realized the government was going to require us to pay several thousand dollars in income tax this year instead of paying us in the form of a credit.

As you can probably imagine, we panicked. Our business had earned a gross income of about $70,000. However, expenses such as wages, gas, vehicle, etc. reduced that figure substantially. Already our net income was much lower than the amount of funds we earned.When we realized we owed taxes, our hearts sank. We began to try to think of every possible expense to reduce our taxable income. Finally, we remembered that we had split the business earlier in the year with our partner. With relief we realized we didn't owe taxes. We were once again going to get a "tax credit." This realization affected our thinking the next year. Instead of making as much money as we could to provide for our family, we got close to the cap and quit. Our contract laborers found themselves without a job. We became trapped and enslaved. There was a glass ceiling that we were scared to break. The welfare state not only harms the richest 1%, by forcing them to pay vast sums into the system, it harms the poorest even more. It steals their desire and ambition.

Government's attempt to "help" has caused more psychological damage than good. Why work harder, when Uncle Sam will subsidize our lack of productivity? The wealthy are robbed of their money, while the poor are robbed of their ambition. I encourage you, if you have not yet; break free from the shackles of government enslavement. This will not only benefit you, but will benefit society as a whole.

Here is an illustration of how the welfare state works:

When I was in 5th grade, I had a teacher named Mr. McLaughlin. Mr. McLaughlin decided to use us, his 5th grade class, for a study. I do not know his intentions or what he thought the results of the study would be. Up until about halfway through the school year, we all worked individually for our own personal grade; but this new idea was to put us in groups and take the highest score from each group as the grade for that entire group. As students we loved it. We thought this meant we would all get better grades.

We were wrong. As a matter of fact, every student's grades went down. After a couple of weeks, Mr. McLaughlin changed the groups to try to get a better result, but nothing he tried worked. Mr. McLaughlin canceled the study rather abruptly just a few weeks into it. Apparently, he did not want our parents to see the outcome of this effort.

We were allowed to choose who would be in our groups the first round. I was blessed and got grouped with John who was a wiz at math and Tammy who had English in her pocket. They were both "straight A" students who never got in trouble. A dream position to be in, I thought.

Unfortunately, it did not work out like it was supposed to. I didn't work as hard because John was good at math. But, John got tired of carrying the rest of us on his back so he didn't work as hard either. That meant John's grade dropped and so did mine. The same happened to Tammy and everyone else in the class. So the groups were changed. However, the outcome did not change. No one was doing as well as we did when we were on our own.

Thankfully, Mr. McLaughlin realized the error and changed his grading methodology back to each student working individually for our own personal grades. Before long John's, Tammy's, and my grades all began to improve. As a matter of fact, the grades of the whole class improved. The reason is that we knew we were responsible for our own work.

We were each capable of doing the work the entire time we were in the groups, but there was no reason to put forth the effort when someone else was willing to do it for us. The result of Mr. McLaughlin's study to some extent illustrates the tendency of many of our neighbors who are on some form of welfare. Many of them could no doubt do better on their own without governmental involvement. Those people who could not improve their lot in life no matter how hard they tried would have the Church to help them. After seeing many people use the government to get whatever they could, I have no doubt that the Church could do a better job than the government does of delivering services to the needy and rejecting those who just want to use the system. After all, it was the Church that originally provided for the less fortunate. The role of government was for protection from enemies foreign and domestic. The role of government has expanded beyond its original purpose and that expansion has resulted in a smaller role for the Church.

CHAPTER 6

LAW AND ORDER

The true reason for government is for protection. Not protection from yourself but from others. When government oversteps its bounds, we should be more than happy to put it back in its place. Unfortunately, we have been late to the game and have lost some liberties already. The more liberties the government takes without citizens doing or saying anything, the more it will continue to take; until, we wake up one morning and realize that we have been put in shackles and chains, maybe for something as ridiculous as having the wrong light bulb in our house.

Some of the proponents of bigger government have spoken in the past of the harsh rules that God placed on the Jews and Christians. The Ten Commandments are nothing in comparison to what Government has placed on us now. Let's take a moment and look at the Ten Commandments:

Exodus 20:1-20 And God spake all these words, saying,2) I am the LORD thy God, which have brought thee out of the land of Egypt, out of the house of bondage.3) Thou shalt have no other gods before me.4) Thou shalt not make unto thee any graven image, or any likeness of any thing that is in heaven above, or that is in the earth beneath, or that is in the water under the earth:5) Thou shalt not bow down thyself to them, nor serve them: for I the LORD thy God am a jealous God, visiting the iniquity of the fathers upon the children unto the third and fourth generation of them that hate me;6) And shewing mercy unto thousands of them that love me, and keep my commandments.7) Thou shalt not take the name of the LORD thy God in vain; for the LORD will not hold him guiltless that taketh his name in vain.8) Remember the sabbath day, to keep it holy.9) Six days shalt thou labour, and do all thy work:10) But the seventh day is the sabbath of the LORD thy God: in it thou shalt not do any work, thou, nor thy son, nor thy daughter, thy manservant, nor thy maidservant, nor thy cattle, nor thy stranger that is within thy gates:11) For in six days the LORD made heaven and earth, the sea, and all that in them is, and rested the seventh day: wherefore the LORD blessed the sabbath day, and hallowed it.12) Honour thy father and thy mother: that thy days may be long upon the land which the LORD thy God giveth thee.13) Thou shalt not kill.14) Thou shalt not commit adultery.15) Thou shalt not steal.16) Thou shalt not bear false witness against thy neighbour.17) Thou shalt not covet thy neighbour's house, thou shalt not covet thy neighbour's wife, nor his manservant, nor his maidservant, nor his ox, nor his ass, nor any thing that is thy neighbour's.18) And all the people saw the thunderings, and the lightnings, and the noise of the trumpet, and the mountain smoking: and when the people saw it, they removed, and stood afar off.19) And they said unto Moses, Speak thou with us, and we will hear: but let not God speak with us, lest we die.20) And Moses said unto the people, Fear not: for God is come to prove you, and that his fear may be before your faces, that ye sin not.

Israel was a theocracy, meaning that the laws and government were directly from God through His chosen messenger, in this case, Moses. The first few commandments were in regard to how the people should respect God and worship Him as their only god. In other words, God should be first in the hearts of His people and they should not worship idols or use God's name in vain. After the first few commandments, God began to give His people instructions on how to behave toward each other.

He instituted a weekend and called the seventh day the Sabbath. He declared that on this day of the week everyone should have a break from work. This commandment applied not only to the store owner, but to the person running the counter. God instructed the people to honor their parents, not to kill, not to commit adultery, not to steal, not to bear false witness, and not to covet someone else's possessions. These seven laws were not to protect the person from himself, but from his neighbor.

Exodus 21:12-36 continues with more detail about God's law concerning how people are to act towards each other.

These laws are all reasonable and do not infringe on the rights of the individual. America was founded on these principles. It is time for a return to the founding documents and the principles cherished by the founding fathers. We do need law and order, but not tyranny. The government of America has grown beyond its usefulness and needs to be reined in.

True law and order comes from the local police, sheriff, and constables not from the federal government. I do not dismiss all government agencies; however, we have allowed these agencies to hijack more power than the founding fathers would have surrendered and tread on liberties that they would have never permitted.

While the government grows and encroaches on us, it does less to protect us. The government, over time, has changed laws to re-victimize victims. The thief sees very little, if any, jail time and pays little to no retribution; while the law abiding citizens are rounded up for practicing their first or second amendment rights. Terrorists are set free and Christians are put on watch lists. Doesn't this seem a little backwards?

If law enforcement, for the most part, was left to the local authorities and the states; I believe we would all be better off. If the federal government would get out of the states and allow them to govern and police themselves; every American would be freer. I encourage all state congresses and governors to tell Washington D.C. to go home and keep your noses out of our respective states. There is only one true reason for a Federal Government and that is to protect us from enemies, foreign and domestic.

CHAPTER 7

STRONG MILITARY

Several years ago, a young lady in the Sunday school class I was attending said one of the most absurd things I had ever heard (until now). We were learning about budgets and practiced making a mock budget for the federal government. This woman cut the military down to nothing and then raised taxes and increased funding for schools and provided free healthcare. Does this sound familiar?

When she shared her team's budget with the class, and argued that this was the best way for government to operate, I could not hold back any longer. I blurted out, "I see, you want a bunch of smart, healthy, dead people."

This seems to be the mindset of many on the Left. They want "free" healthcare, "free" college education, but want no funds to go towards the one thing that the federal government was originally set up to do. An inadequate military budget will eventually result in either a devastating loss of life due to an attack on our nation or the enslavement of our people by an enemy with a way of life that is inconsistent with freedom or it may result in both. I choose to accept neither.

Ezekiel tells of a story about an army that brought peace. The hand of the Lord was upon Ezekiel and took him out in the Spirit to the middle of a valley which was full of bones. The Spirit then made him pass around the perimeter of the valley of bones. There were many bones in the valley and they were very dry. The Lord then asked him if the bones could live. Ezekiel gave a fantastic answer. He said, "Lord God, thou knowst." Then the Lord told him to prophesy to the bones and tell them to hear the word of the Lord. Say to the bones, the Lord continued, "Behold, I will cause breath to enter into you, and ye shall live: and I will lay sinews upon you, and will bring up flesh upon you, and cover you with skin, and put breath in you, and ye shall live; and ye shall know that I am the Lord."

So Ezekiel prophesied as God had told him. As he was prophesying he heard a noise and there was a shaking and the bones began to come together. When he looked, the sinews and flesh came on the bones and the skin covered them, but there was no breath in them.

Then the Lord said to him, "Prophesy unto the wind, prophesy, son of man, and say to the wind, "Thus saith the Lord God; Come from the four winds, O breath, and breathe upon these slain, that they may live." And so Ezekiel prophesied as the Lord had commanded him, and the breath came into them and they lived. They then stood on their feet, an exceeding great army. (Ezekiel 37:1-10)

In verse 26, the Lord tells Ezekiel that He would make a covenant of peace with Israel, and that it would be an everlasting covenant. He further states that He would place them in a good land, multiply them, and would put His sanctuary in the middle of them forever. (Ezekiel 37:26)

There is no bigger proponent for peace than I. This is the reason, I support a strong military. There was no peace for

God's people until the "exceeding great army" was revived. Some call for peace while demanding a dismantling of the military. This is the surest way to invite a bully nation to push our country around.

I grew up with siblings who were almost always in some kind of quarrel. They thought they were tough. One day, my older brother found himself in a fight with a neighbor boy. My brother grabbed a stick and began to charge the neighbor. Someone made a comment about him using a stick, so, to show that he was a "man," he gave the stick to the neighbor. Well, you guessed it; the neighbor boy did not mind what the other kids thought and began to swing the stick at my brother. The neighbor won the fight that day.

There are countries in the world that don't care what other nations think. They will use whatever is in their grasp to attain victory. Other countries are bullies who claim to be peaceful but provide the "stick" to countries who don't mind being seen as bullies or rejoice when those countries find a stick on their own (nuclear bomb.)

Imagine that you have a five year old daughter who goes into the backyard to play. While she is in the backyard, a thirteen year old boy jumps the wooden fence and threatens your daughter with a knife. When she comes screaming into the house, does it make sense to sit down with her to explain what she did wrong and why she should apologize to the boy making him want to act in such a way? This is the response from some in politics today.

People have come into our country and threatened our lives and liberty. Some of the people who are supposed to protect us have decided to psychoanalyze what happened, and are now blaming our country for the attack against us.

This incident (boy pulling out knife) actually happened in my home. My response, however, was much different. When my daughter came screaming into the house, I strapped on my .45 and begun to stroll around in the backyard. The boy had already jumped back across the fence and within a few minutes a car skid up to the neighbor's house. A voice from inside the car called out to the boy, "Are you trying to get yourself killed? GET IN!" We never had another problem with that boy.

When war is declared on this nation, whether from another nation or Muslim extremists; we need to strap on our .45 as a nation and take a stroll. In the war on terror, some who hold high positions in our government have acted fearfully. They have not wanted to bomb certain sights, because it might make our enemy upset. What? You've got to be kidding me.

When the men flew the planes into the twin towers, and the Pentagon, and crashed landed in the Pennsylvania field; they had a message for America. The message was a hatred for our country and our way of life. The hatred that caused these terrorist to act is shared by many Muslim extremist who support their effort. They were clear on their goal. When we go to war, we need one goal: WIN! Our operations should be geared to killing the enemy, forcing them to surrender and causing them to regret the day they thought they could make America buckle.

America's leaders need to put aside political correctness and the feelings of the enemy and kick their tails. When the enemy wakes up in the morning, one of the first thoughts that should go through their minds should be a question, "will I live to see tonight?" Bullies only respect strength. If we want peace, we will find it in a strong military and an armed citizenry.

Tactics

Gratefully, our military excels at tactics, technology, and technical warfare. The book of Judges gives us an account of what good can be done tactically.

When Gideon was about to go to war, the Lord told him that his army was too big to allow God to give Gideon the victory. God's primary reason for this unusual observation was that Israel would think they won the battle by their own strength instead of God's strength. You've got to remember, God does not think like we do. His ways are above our ways as far as the heavens are above the earth. So, the Lord told Gideon that he needed to send home all those soldiers who were afraid.

The crazy thing is that twenty two thousand people left due to fear! Only ten thousand men stayed to fight. The Lord then said to Gideon, "The people are yet too many; bring them down unto the water, and I will try them for thee there: and it shall be, that of whom I say unto thee, This shall go with thee, the same shall go with thee; and of whomsoever I say unto thee, this shall not go with thee, the same shall not go."

So Gideon took the people to the water, and the Lord told him to separate the ones that lapped the water up like a dog and the ones that bowed down on their knees to drink.

There were three hundred men that lapped the water, putting their hand to their mouth, but the rest bowed down on their knees to drink the water. The Lord then told Gideon that He would give him victory by using the three hundred men. So Gideon let the remainder of his army go and kept only the three hundred men.

Besides wanting His people's total trust and dependence, God had other reasons for His decision to have Gideon send home those that were afraid and those that got down on their knees to drink. During war, each soldier's life depends on his fellow soldiers. Every soldier needs to know that the man standing next to him is confident and capable of fighting for the cause and for his fellow soldier's life. If a soldier is afraid or is on his knees when the enemy approaches, he will not be able to draw his sword or defend himself.

However, none of Gideon's army ended up needing a sword for the battle. The army of three hundred men surrounded the camp of the enemy. Their "weapons" were trumpets, vessels, and lights. They put the vessels over the lights and when they were in place around the enemy, they raised the trumpets to their mouths, blew and broke the vessels. When the enemy heard the trumpets they thought legions of military men had surrounded them. Their thoughts seemed to be confirmed when they looked up and saw lights all around their camp. The enemy panicked and turned on each other. They killed their fellow soldier. We would call this type of war psychological warfare. It is still used today. Engaging in psychological attacks reduces expense and amount of resources that would otherwise be required to be victorious. (Paraphrased from Judges Chapter 7)

However, psychological warfare only works if you are able to deceive the enemy into submission. The Left uses this tactic all the time by telling conservatives that we are the minority and that our ideas belong in the 1800's. We become quiet and begin to think that we are alone. We are deceived and then submit to their agenda. For the most part, the psychological attacks employed by the Left have worked.

The Left speaks of reducing our country's military power and increasing the use of diplomacy. The lessons of Scripture show us that diplomacy only works when it is supported by military strength. Lack of military strength and the fortitude to use it is one reason that President Carter's administration could not achieve the release of the hostages held in Iran. It took President Reagan's determination and commitment to do whatever it took to free these Americans to convince the Iranians it was in their best interest to cooperate.

Diplomacy is appropriate and helpful when accompanied by strength. The story of Gideon illustrates proper use of diplomacy. Gideon took a servant with him and listened outside the tent to some of the enemy's army. They spoke of their fear of being annihilated by the army of the Israelites. This fear became a great tool in Gideon's hands. Though Scripture compares the enemy to grasshoppers in the field, because of their great number, victory would belong to Gideon.

The United States of America must maintain a military that is second to none. The Islamic extremists should fear us, communists should fear us, fascists should fear us, and so should any that would consider attacking our country.

When we reduce our military strength, remove military presence from nations that have demonstrated a will to attack our country and were in favor of attacking us, and play political correctness with nations that have called war on us, we are telling our enemies that we do not have the stomach required to maintain our liberties. This is the wrong message to send to the rest of the world. I believe in diplomacy; however, I believe in diplomacy that works. And diplomacy only works from a position of strength.

Diplomacy

Diplomacy works well if you can back up your words with actions. In the book of Exodus, Moses and Aaron spoke to the Pharaoh and told him to let God's people go. Obviously,

Pharaoh did not know who the God of Israel was so he refused to release them. Moses and Aaron then asked the Pharaoh to let the Israelites leave for three days so they could make a sacrifice to the Lord. If he refused, the Lord would fall on Egypt with pestilence or the sword. Again, Pharaoh's heart was hardened and he told them he would make the labors of the Israelites, who were his slaves, more difficult. Pharaoh fulfilled this promise by making the slaves gather the straw required to construct the bricks they were ordered to make every day. Prior to this time, the laborers were able to use straw gathered by the task masters. (Paraphrased from Exodus 5:1-7)

In Exodus chapter 6 verse 1, the Lord said to Moses, "Now shalt thou see what I will do to Pharaoh: for with a strong hand shall he let them go, and with a strong hand shall he drive them out of his land."

The following excerpt from Exodus illustrates the fact that strength always supports effective diplomacy. Some elites would tell us that we should show "good faith" and reduce our country's military strength. However we can clearly see from the Scripture that Pharaoh did not relinquish even after nine terrible plagues. It was not until the tenth plague of death that he finally let Israel go.

Exodus 12:28-31 And the children of Israel went away, and did as the LORD had commanded Moses and Aaron, so did they.29) And it came to pass, that at midnight the LORD smote all the firstborn in the land of Egypt, from the firstborn of Pharaoh that sat on his throne unto the firstborn of the captive that was in the dungeon; and all the firstborn of cattle.30) And Pharaoh rose up in the night, he, and all his servants, and all the Egyptians; and there was a great cry in Egypt; for there was not a house where there was not one dead.31) And he called for Moses and Aaron by night, and said, Rise up, and get you forth from among my people, both ye and the children of Israel; and go, serve the LORD, as ye have said.

Diplomacy is limited by the strength one has and is willing to use. Without military strength, diplomacy will never be able to destroy tyranny; any nation that attempts diplomacy without military strength will become a slave to the tyrant. Exodus goes on to talk about the Egyptians pursuit of Israel:

Exodus 14:23-28 And the Egyptians pursued, and went in after them to the midst of the sea, even all Pharaoh's horses, his chariots, and his horsemen.24) And it came to pass, that in the morning watch the LORD looked unto the host of the Egyptians through the pillar of fire and of the cloud, and troubled the host of the Egyptians,25) And took off their chariot wheels, that they drave them heavily: so that the Egyptians said, Let us flee from the face of Israel; for the LORD fighteth for them against the Egyptians.26) And the LORD said unto Moses, Stretch out thine hand over the sea, that the waters may come again upon the Egyptians, upon their chariots, and upon their horsemen.27) And Moses stretched forth his hand over the sea, and the sea returned to his strength when the morning appeared; and the Egyptians fled against it; and the LORD overthrew the Egyptians in the midst of the sea.28) And the waters returned, and covered the chariots, and the horsemen, and all the host of Pharaoh that came into the sea after them; there remained not so much as one of them.

Tyrants never give up, they pursue to the ends of the world. In August of 1776, Benjamin Franklin coined the phrase, "Rebellion to tyrants is obedience to God." He was comparing the Exodus of Israel from Egypt to the overthrowing of English rule in the United States of America.

Tyranny not only comes from forces outside our country, but it can lurk in local and state governments and certainly can exist within the federal government as well. This is why our country must maintain a strong military and an armed citizenry.

CHAPTER 8

RIGHT TO BEAR ARMS

There is a dance that the Left plays with our liberties. They take some portion of our liberties away. We complain. They give us back a little. We rejoice because we get a little liberty back and forget about the liberties that were not returned.

It is like a magician who asks you for your watch and wallet so he can make them disappear. We become upset, so the magician magically makes the watch reappear. Now, we are appeased because we have our watch back and we have entirely forgotten about our wallet.

Giving us back some of the rights they took away is not enough. I want ALL my rights back. Calling them privileges is a misuse of the term. They are not privileges, they are rights. By changing the word, they change the argument. For instance, it should be a right to drive, but now we call it a privilege. So, if driving is a privilege, the government can determine who can and who can't drive regardless of any criminal activity. What I mean is, if you were at fault in an accident you could lose your right to drive. But now they can take away your "privilege" to drive for whatever reason they please.

Those in power on the left have done the same thing with guns. Now it is a privilege to be able to bear (carry) arms. The Constitution did not call it a privilege, but guaranteed it as a right. I have heard some Christians question whether or not Jesus would have had a gun or would have let His disciples carry guns. In Matthew Chapter 26, verse 51, the Bible says that one of them (Disciples) "stretched out his hand, and drew his sword . . ." John said in Chapter 18 verse 10, "Then Simon Peter having a sword drew it, and smote the high priest's servant . . ." Peter had his own sword. At one point, Jesus sent the disciples out to minister in the surrounding area and told them not to worry about money, what they would say, or even about their shoes. In the Book of Luke, He asked them if they lacked anything, and they said they lacked nothing. Then Jesus said, "But now, he that hath a purse, let him take it, and likewise his scrip: and he that hath no sword, let him sell his garment, and buy one." (Paraphrased from Luke 22:35-38)

Did you catch that? Jesus told His disciples that a sword was more important to them than their garments! Jesus gives another illustration:

Luke 11:21 When a strong man armed keepeth his palace, his goods are in peace:

Jesus gives the answer to peace and security: arming the homeowner. Gun control proponents miss a small detail in their argument: by making laws that take the gun out of the hand of the law abiding citizen, we guarantee the criminal free rein with his. We in effect bind the strong man of the house and announce to the lawless the vulnerability of the innocent. However, if we keep the strong man armed, his goods will remain in peace.

The founding fathers of this nation laid a foundation that still holds to this day. The Constitution contains an amendment that guarantees citizens the "right to keep and bear arms." Why was this amendment placed into the Constitution, what was meant by a "well-regulated militia," and what would the elimination of this right potentially mean to our society? Was this "right" to bear arms meant only for the soldiers of the militia or was it meant for the people in general? What is the significance of an armed or a disarmed populace? Using history as a point of reference, we will reevaluate the right to keep and bear arms.

On March 5th, 1770 a standing British army was surrounded by approximately 400 Bostonians. These Bostonians were already enraged due to a decree by the British government stating that the people must furnish quarters to British soldiers.

These colonists began to antagonize the British "Red Coats" saying things like, "Come on you rascals, you bloody backs, you lobster scoundrels, fire if you dare, G-d damn you, fire and be damned, we know you dare not." (*Boston Massacre Historical Society*). They were so close they struck the soldiers muskets with clubs. Before the end of the day, three Bostonians were dead, and two more would follow them to the grave due to the eruption of violence on that fateful day.

The Boston Massacre set the fear of a standing British army or any standing army in the hearts of the colonists. The passion of the American patriots furthered the cause for the second amendment to the Bill of Rights (*CQ Encyclopedia of American Government, Library of Congress*). "The colonists also developed a healthy mistrust for standing armies-that is, military forces composed solely of professional soldiers and controlled by a central government." According to Gordon Witkin and Katia Hetter in, *The Fight to Bear Arms.* (1995).

The wary view of standing armies can be illustrated by the North Carolina Constitution. The North Carolina Constitution of 1776 states, "That the people have a right to bear arms, for the defense of the State; and as standing armies, in times of peace, are dangerous to liberty, they ought not to be kept up; and that the military should be kept under strict subordination to, and governed by, the civil power." (Volokh, Eugene. n.d.)

If this text is to be taken in the strictest form, the North Carolina Constitution separates a standing army from the military. It further implies that a standing army (professional soldiers . . . controlled by a central government) should only be allowed in a time of war.

The idea at the time the Constitution was written was that if the populace was armed; there would be less need for a standing army. Times have changed since the Constitution was written; now men are able to fly. Therefore, there is the possible danger of attacks from the air that men on the ground would be defenseless against. Realizing this, I see the need for an air force, navy, and marines. However, a standing army on our soil is a thing to be feared by all liberty loving Americans, and in today's political climate, Christians should be especially wary.

The second amendment to the United States Constitution states, "A well-regulated militia, being necessary to the security of a Free State, the right of the people to keep and bear arms, shall not be infringed." (United States Constitution) There has arisen a controversy due to the wording of the second Amendment. Who has the right to bear arms? Is it the militia (National Guard) or the people? According to the *Reader's Digest Great Encyclopedic Dictionary*, (1966) a militia is "any able-bodied man from the age of eighteen to forty five and not currently in the military, who is, however, subject to being called in the event of an emergency." According to the *Grolier Multimedia Encyclopedia*, (2005) a militia is now what we would call the National Guard. Would there ever be a time when we (Americans) might need a militia again?

Alexander Hamilton wrote in the *Federalist Papers* about the use of militias, stating that there may come a time when a militia from another state would need to enter a neighboring state to stop either an insurrection or invasion. (*Federalist Papers*, 1961 edition)

The question remains, to whom does the right to bear arms apply: the militia or the people? This debate was addressed by Bruce Gold (2002). Gold states that in colonial times, men were nervous about an "overpowering federal government". He surmises that this fear made the second amendment crucial, not only for a militia, but for the individual. He claims the founding fathers saw the "need to reassert the individual right to keep and bear arms by including it in certain 'declaratory and restrictive clauses.'"

The sentiment asserted by Bruce Gold to have guided the crafting of the second amendment of United States Constitution, is evident in many of the state constitutions as well.

Professor Eugene Volokh has compiled a list of states and amendments that acknowledge the people's "right to bear arms." Though these amendments do change from time to time, the intent remains the same. The following states have reaffirmed the wording and their view of the second amendment of the United States Constitution:

> 1776, North Carolina; 1776, Pennsylvania; 1777, Vermont; 1780, Massachusetts; 1792, Kentucky; 1796, Tennessee; 1802, Ohio; 1816, Indiana; 1817, Mississippi;

1818, Connecticut; 1819, Maine; 1819, Alabama; 1820, Missouri; 1835, Michigan; 1836 and 1845, Texas; 1836, Arkansas; 1838, Florida; 1842, Rhode Island; 1857, Oregon; 1859, Kansas; 1865, Georgia; 1876, Colorado, 1879, Louisiana; 1885, Washington; 1889, Wyoming; 1889, South Dakota; 1889, Montana; 1889, Idaho; 1895, South Carolina; 1896, Utah; 1907, Oklahoma; 1912, Arizona; 1912, New Mexico; 1959, Hawaii; 1959, Alaska; 1970, Illinois; 1971, Virginia; 1982, Nevada; 1982, New Hampshire; 1984, North Dakota; 1986, West Virginia; 1987, Delaware; 1988, Nebraska; 1998, Wisconsin.

Of the fifty states that comprise the United States, forty four of them have amendments that secure the right to bear arms (88% of the states) in their constitutions. The six states that do not have amendments with the right to bear arms simply refer to the United States Constitution.

Though these states support the right to bear arms, dating back to the late 1800's several of them regulated the ownership and transporting of such arms. However, the past two decades have seen a shift in the political landscape. This shift has brought to the forefront a new concept. In more than twenty-six states, a legal resident, who qualifies, may obtain a permit to carry a concealed weapon on his/her person (*www.keepandbeararms.com*)

Did this deregulation of an armed citizenry create a rise in crime? The short answer is no. As a matter of fact, with deregulation has come a decrease in violent crime. During the same period, nations with increasingly restrictive gun laws and regulations are experiencing increasing rates of violent crime. In a study of violent crime and the legal possession of firearms in America versus the more restrictive policies of England/Wales, and Australia we can clearly see the difference between the registering and regulating of firearms and the deregulation of firearms done in America.

Violent Crime Rates

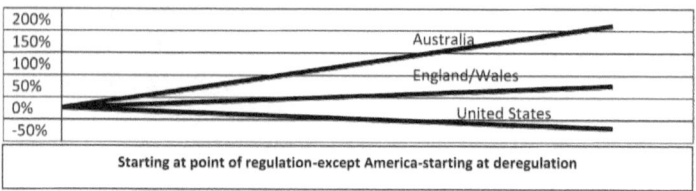

Violent crime increased in Australia by 166%, from 1997 to 2003, when new legislation was passed to regulate the registration and ownership of guns. The homicide rate in England/Wales jumped 50% and gun crime increased by 35%. The United States stands out in the trends set by these more regulated nations: violent crime fell by 42% since the introduction of conceal carry laws. (Mauser, 2003)

These startling statistics have not ended the debate. The second amendment to the Constitution continues to be raised as a point of contention. We are told that in most cases, the United States Supreme Court clearly determines the constitutionality of laws and actions that are brought before it. However, on the second amendment, the Supreme Court has been, for the most part, silent. Even the cases on which the Court has ruled, such as *The United States v. Miller*, the question of an individual right versus collective rights to bear arms is not sufficiently addressed.

The Miller case was a question of registration. Can the government force its citizens to register sawed off shot guns? Miller won in the lower courts; however, he failed to appear when the federal government took the case to the

Supreme Court. "The Supreme Court ruled in his absence; however after the ruling, there was still no resolution." In other words, after the ruling, there was still no resolution between the individual rights and the collective rights of the people. (Bradbury, S., Marshal, C., Nielson, H) This has left the question of the second amendment to be resolved in the political arena. Did the drafters of the Constitution intend for individual citizens to bear arms or rather for government-controlled militia to be the only bearers of arms?

Besides increasing rates of violent crime, what would be the other consequences of disarming of the citizenry? Is the rise in crime, such as in Australia and England/Wales, the only points of statistical relevance or does history illustrate a more deviant potential?

During the Nazi regime of the 1930s and early 40s there was a call for the disarmament of the Jewish population. This disarmament extended not only to the Jews but to all of the people of Germany and those of occupied Europe.

The registration of gun ownership in the European nations served as a convenient tool to the Nazi party. When the Nazi Party entered Czechoslovakia and Poland in 1938, they found it easy to disarm the public due to the national registration of firearms. Robert Jackson, attorney General of the United States in 1941, asked Congress for a national registration of firearms. Seeing the events in Europe, Congress refused such a request. (*Halbrook, S., 2001*)

Though this argument appears far from over, American history, a study of statistics, and world history all illuminate the importance of this issue. Alexander Hamilton wrote of the tendency to relinquish rights due to fear. In the *Federalist Papers*, he wrote:

Safety from external danger is the most powerful director of national conduct. Even the ardent love of liberty will, after time, give way to its dictates. The violent destruction of life and property incident to war, the continual effort and alarm attendant on a state of continual danger, will compel nations the most attached to liberty to resort for repose and security to institutions which have a tendency to destroy their civil and political rights. To be more safe, they at length become willing to run the risk of being less free. (1961 edition)

Time has proven Hamilton correct. However, I am one who resents and despises every law that is implemented under the guise of safety, while it steals my freedom. Let me be less safe and more free. Patrick Henry's famous words echo in my heart: "Give me liberty or give me death." Benjamin Franklin referred to this type of scenario when he spoke about those that would give up their liberty for security. He stated that people who are willing to make this trade "Deserve neither liberty nor security." (www.ushistory.org/franklin/quotable/quote04.htm)

The era of emotional decision-making by those who hold political powers, needs to come to an end. The necessity of an armed citizenry is clearly painted by history. Using the events of the past, we have observed the tendency for tyrannies to rise, freedom to be extinguished, and the human spirit to be crushed under the guise of safety (a disarmed public). However, when men and women are allowed to defend themselves and their neighbors by the possession and bearing of arms, tyranny is kept at bay, violent crime subsides, and freedom is preserved.

The founders fought for and designed our Constitution to maintain a limited government, not a shackled citizenry. The founders were less concerned about foreign invasions than they were about the encroachment of our own government on the freedoms of Americans. Freedom itself is the primary reason for an armed public.

CHAPTER 9

ABORTION

In the Declaration of Independence Thomas Jefferson wrote, "We hold these truths to be self-evident, that all men are created equal, that they are endowed by their Creator with certain unalienable Rights, that among these are Life, Liberty and the pursuit of Happiness."

So far, I have spent a lot of time dealing with liberty, without which there is no happiness; however, liberty is useless without life. There should probably be no issue more important to the Christian than that of life. All other liberties blossom from the first tenet: Life. If the denying of the unalienable right of life is permitted by society, then all other rights are placed in question. Don't get me wrong, Christians ought to be outspoken about each liberty and every right that is stolen from us by an over-extended government. However, we are morally required to speak out on the foundational issue of life.

Long ago, a teenage girl about 13 or 14 years old discovered she was pregnant. The child was not her boyfriend's and she and her boyfriend both knew it could not possibly be. She knew she risked losing her boyfriend when he found out about the pregnancy. In those days, a single mother would be shunned and have no prospect of supporting herself and the child. If she lost her boyfriend, not only would she lose his future income, she would lose any hope for a stable secure environment for her child and herself. Now she was faced with a decision. Should she abort her baby or should she just tell her boyfriend the truth and hope that he understands? If your answer was abort, you have killed the Savior of all mankind. This scenario plays out in our communities every day. What impact can that one child make if only he or she is allowed to live? One potentially abortion-minded teenager and her un-aborted child changed the course of civilization forever.

The Book of Luke records the visit of the angel Gabriel who was sent from God into the city of Nazareth in the region of Galilee. The angel went to a virgin who was espoused to a man named Joseph, who came from the house and lineage of Israel's beloved King David. The virgin's name was Mary. The angel said to Mary, "Hail, thou that art highly favored, the Lord is with thee: blessed art thou among women." When Mary saw the angel, she was troubled by what he said, and wondered what this greeting meant. The angel told her not to fear, because she had found favor with God. Gabriel then told Mary that she would conceive and give birth to a son and that his name would be Jesus. Gabriel continued, "He shall be great, and shall be called the Son of the Highest: and the Lord God shall give unto him the throne of his father David: and he shall reign over the house of Jacob forever; and of his kingdom there shall be no end." Understandably, Mary had a question or two, "How shall this be, seeing I know not a man?" The angel then gave her the word, "The Holy Ghost shall come upon thee, and the power of the highest shall overshadow thee: therefore also that holy thing which shall be born of thee shall be called the Son of God." (Paraphrased from Luke 1:26-35)

Matthew also gives an account of the Savior's birth when he writes:

> Matthew 1:18-25 Now the birth of Jesus Christ was on this wise: When as his mother Mary was espoused to Joseph, before they came together, she was found with child of the Holy Ghost. 19) Then Joseph her husband, being a just *man,* and not willing to make her a publick example, was minded to put her away privily. 20) But while he thought on these things, behold, the angel of the Lord appeared unto him in a dream, saying, Joseph, thou son of David, fear not to take unto thee Mary thy wife: for that which is conceived in her is of the Holy Ghost. 21) And she shall bring forth a son, and thou shalt call his name JESUS: for he shall save his people from their sins. 22) Now all this was done, that it might be fulfilled which was spoken of the Lord by the prophet, saying, 23) Behold, a virgin shall be with child, and shall bring forth a son, and they shall call his name Emmanuel, which being interpreted is, God with us.24) Then Joseph being raised from sleep did as the angel of the Lord had bidden him, and took unto him his wife: 25) And knew her not till she had brought forth her firstborn son: and he called his name JESUS.

Mary risked losing her fiancé and even her life, yet she still chose to give birth to the child that she carried. Joseph had the chance to choose another course in his life and walk away, yet he chose to stay. He raised Jesus as his own. Though Joseph bore no genetic responsibility for the baby that Mary carried, he chose to stay with her. There is something to be said about those men who are more than sperm donors. They are true men who stick around and love their wives and children, regardless of whether the children are biologically theirs or not. And there is something to be said about the mothers who choose life, regardless of the obstacles they may face. Parents who choose to give life, even and maybe especially those who give infertile couples a chance to love and raise an adopted child are heroes.

Ronald Reagan wrote a book entitled *Abortion and the Conscience of a Nation*, while he was President. I strongly encourage you to read it. I could never do it justice, so rather than plagiarizing his work, I will just encourage you to read it; and present to you relevant passages from Scriptures along with some of my personal thoughts.

Scripture is clear about life. We see in the Old Testament that the law applies to life from the point of conception and not merely after birth.

Exodus 21:22-25 If men strive, and hurt a woman with child, so that her fruit depart *from her*, and yet no mischief follow: he shall be surely punished, according as the woman's husband will lay upon him; and he shall pay as the judges *determine*. 23) And if *any* mischief follow, then thou shalt give life for life, 24) Eye for eye, tooth for tooth, hand for hand, foot for foot, 25) Burning for burning, wound for wound, stripe for stripe.

The term "fruit depart" meant early birth or premature birth; "mischief" meant the death of the child, "life for life" meant that the death penalty was required of anyone who took the life of an unborn child. The Left has told us for years that the baby in the womb is merely tissue, not life. If this is how God looks at it, then why would He require the death penalty for anyone who causes a woman to abort? It is clear that God does not consider the unborn child to be "just tissue." Further scriptural references to life in the womb follow:

> Job 31:15 Did not he that made me in the womb make him? and did not one fashion us in the womb?

The same God that formed us, formed that child yet unborn. Our mothers either loved us enough, or respected God and life enough to give us the opportunity to have life. Wouldn't it be right to give the unborn the same choice we had?

> Psalm 22:8-10 He trusted on the LORD *that* he would deliver him: let him deliver him, seeing he delighted in him. 9) But thou *art* he that took me out of the womb: thou didst make me hope *when I was* upon my mother's breasts. 10) I was cast upon thee from the womb: thou *art* my God from my mother's belly.

The psalmist declares that God is, "He that took me out of the womb." As God is the author and creator of all life, He is also the sustainer of it. This explains how Jesus can be the Great Physician. God gave reason to hope while we were yet suckling. The psalmist declared that God was his God from his mother's belly. In other words, from my beginnings God was there. It is my firm belief that every child is a blessing from God, regardless of the environment into which the child is born.

> Isaiah 44:2 Thus saith the LORD that made thee, and formed thee from the womb, *which* will help thee; Fear

not, O Jacob, my servant; and thou, Jesurun, whom I have chosen.

The Lord does not claim to make us from birth, but from the womb.

> Isaiah 49:1 Listen, O isles, unto me; and hearken, ye people, from far; The LORD hath called me from the womb; from the bowels of my mother hath he made mention of my name.

God knows the child by name that is in his or her mother's womb. Paul wrote in Romans11:29, "For the gifts and calling of God are without repentance." God has a calling on each child for which He will not repent. In other words, God plans every child, yet the mother holds the life and future of God's will in her hand (womb).

There are those who say God's will has to be done: that His will is forced to be executed on earth. If this were the case, why would Jesus use these words teaching his disciples to pray: "Thy kingdom come. Thy will be done in earth, as it is in heaven." (Matthew 6:10) If God's will was going to be done no matter what, this prayer was a waste of time and energy. In 2 Peter, we read, "The Lord is not slack concerning his promise, as some men count slackness; but is longsuffering to us-ward, not willing that any should perish, but that all should come to repentance." (2Peter 3:9) If God's will is "forced" and He is not willing that any should perish, then it would be impossible to be lost. If it is impossible to be lost, why repent or believe?

This makes it apparent that it is possible to thwart the will of God. Every time an abortion occurs, the will of God is abandoned and left undone.

Isaiah 49:15 Can a woman forget her sucking child, that she should not have compassion on the son of her womb? yea, they may forget, yet will I not forget thee.

In America today, each new mother is told not to consider, much less have compassion on, the "son of her womb." If she already has several children or is financially strained, she is advised to remove the child from existence. In the scripture just quoted, God asked the question, can a mother forget her sucking child? He then answers the question by saying that even if a mother can forget her own offspring, He will not forget.

Jeremiah 1:5 Before I formed thee in the belly I knew thee; and before thou camest forth out of the womb I sanctified thee, *and* I ordained thee a prophet unto the nations.

God's Word tells us that He knows us even before He forms us. It says that He sanctifies us before our mothers give birth to us. This means that when a mother destroys her child, she is destroying a sanctified life known by God. How many prophets, doctors, or great leaders has the Lord ordained for America that we have allowed to be extinguished?

Luke 1:41 And it came to pass, that, when Elisabeth heard the salutation of Mary, the babe leaped in her womb; and Elisabeth was filled with the Holy Ghost:

Here we see that John the Baptist experienced emotion in the womb. Was John the only child who felt emotion in the womb? Have you ever seen a sonogram in which the child is sucking his or her thumb? Why does a child suck their thumb? It is a comforting action. Why would there be a need for comfort in the womb if there was no emotion?

> Deuteronomy 30:19 I call heaven and earth to record this day against you, *that* I have set before you life and death, blessing and cursing: therefore choose life, that both thou and thy seed may live:

The Lord has made it clear. Life is sacred upon its creation and life is created by God at the moment of conception. God doesn't play politics, but He has made clear His position on the question of abortion. God is most definitely prolife. This is not a Republican or Democratic issue or an issue of right and left; this is an issue of right and wrong. It is often the easiest way out to kill those who don't have a voice. But if America will ever secure individual rights and protect human dignity again, the Christian Right must speak loudly and clearly on the issue of life.

CHAPTER 10

ANIMAL RIGHTS/ ENVIRONMENTALISM

It amazes me that many who are pro-choice when it comes to killing children are not pro-choice when it comes to humans having dominion over God's creation. This is despite the fact that God declared in the book of Genesis that He made man in His own image and blessed them and instructed them to be fruitful, multiply, replenish the earth, and to subdue it. He also told them to have dominion over everything that is living and moves on the earth. God gave man every herb bearing seed, every tree, every beast of the earth, every fowl of the air, and everything that creeps on the earth. (Genesis 1:27-30)

God gave man dominion over the animals, not animals dominion over man. This is one of the primary reasons the Left fights so hard to keep Creationism and Intelligent Design out of our public schools, while they promote Darwinism and Evolution. If there is really no difference between a human being and a monkey or if people truly evolved from tadpoles, it logically follows that killing any animal for any reason is equivalent to murder.

While liberal animal-rights activists tell us the lives of all types of animal species are too critical to risk, their true agenda is apparent in their inflexible application of the same approach to their concerns. If the animal-rights groups truly wanted to save animals, they would be looking at alternative solutions to the ones they currently employ. The way to save species of animals is to find ways for people to profit from their preservation. Have you wondered why we do not have a shortage of cows, pigs, or chickens? The reason is simple; man has learned how to make a profit from these animals. Steaks, milk, pork and poultry have been the driving force and the catalyst to the longevity of these animals.

In Texas there are ranches that profit from exotic animals. Animals that are either endangered or extinct in Africa are thriving in Texas. What is the secret? The secret is profit. Up to ten percent of the animals are hunted every year. Hunters on these ranches pay dearly for the privilege. Today, there are more than a quarter million exotic animals in Texas along with more than 125 different endangered species.

However, there are those who proclaim that killing any animal is wrong, even if the establishment of wild animal preserves which allow hunting leads to a net gain in the population of endangered animal species on the earth. There are those who say that African animals belong in Africa, knowing that these animals are extinct in their natural habitat. These so-called animal-rights-activists would rather see a species become extinct than have them hunted, but thriving in Texas.

(http://www.tmdailypost.com/article/animals/video-60-minutes-exotic-game-ranches-texas)

By the actions of many on the left who claim to have the interests at heart, we are able to deduce that saving the animal is not their main objective. The real objective is control. You read right. Regardless of their claims, the animal—rights and environmental movements are not about what they purport, they are all about control.

As part of the agenda of those supposedly focused on the environment, something such as the discovery of a tadpole in a spring, translates into the people not being allowed to drink the spring's water. Once again these groups put the needs of animals over the needs and rights of people in order to exert control over the people. Similarly, the discovery of a rat in a field means that the farmer who owns the field cannot work the field for fear of disrupting the habitat of the rat. Through actions such as these, those engineering the animal-rights movement gain control over entire communities and groups of businesses such as the farmer in the example above. So, then the rights of the people and the farmer are usurped. Yet, no one stands up for the farmer who has lost the use of his field, or the people who must find another source of water even though they live directly over a perfectly good source, now. Who is safe from the reach of these people?

This political movement, for that is what this ideology has become, is able to control where businesses open, where people live, and what people can do on their own property. This is in direct contrast to what the founding fathers had in mind when they set up this great Nation. Many of the people who wield this great power and make these critical decisions hold no elected offices and are not representative of or accountable to the people.

Animal—rights activists are joined in their quest for power by another group: environmentalists. Environmentalists have the same objective, but espouse another ideology to reach that goal. Instead of using animals to gain power, they use nature or the environment. Many animal—rights activists are also environmentalists.

Environmentalists are the ones who warned us about global warming until it was shown that the world was not getting warmer. Now they proclaim the dangers of global climate change instead. Environmentalists blamed the world's increasing temperature on almost every activity in which human beings engaged from driving to breathing.

As you are reading this book, you might find it surprising that I am a believer in the theory of global warming. I believe global warming is a reality. It is induced by pollution and it is man-made. However, the kind of warming I am witnessing is not a result of smog, carbon dioxide, or the number of humans living on the earth. The solution to the type of global warming that is of primary concern can be found in the Book of Revelation:

> Revelation 16:8 And the fourth angel poured out his vial upon the sun; and power was given unto him to scorch men with fire.9) And men were scorched with great heat, and blasphemed the name of God, which hath power over these plagues: and they repented not to give him glory.

The dire threat of the global warming that could destroy our earth is a result of un-repented sin. If you want to do your part to help the environment and prevent global warming, the answers are simple: repent and give God the glory. That is most likely not the answer most environmentalists would like to hear. The reason they do not want to hear the true solution to the problem is two—fold. First, they do not want to subject themselves to any higher Authority, and second, they do not want to release their environmental "cause" with which they are able to control the masses.

As Christians, we believe that God spoke and said, "Let there be lights in the firmament of the heavens to divide the day from the night; and let them be for signs, and for seasons, and for days, and years." (Genesis 1:14)

In other words, God established day and night, created the seasons, and established the earth's movement around the sun within the span of a year. Since God created the seasons, He chose for the weather to change seasonally. Thus we experience summer, winter, autumn, and spring.

If the changes in the weather are orchestrated by God, then those who tell us it is our fault the climate is changing have replaced God with man. The real explanation for global climate change is God, but the Left cannot acknowledge that because in so doing, they would have to acknowledge that God exists and exerts His authority over life on earth. If the Left acknowledged there is a God who is in control of the weather, that would mean man cannot significantly affect the earth's temperature. If the Left admits that it is not man who causes the climate to change, they will lose the ability to control the populace through fear. Therefore, they must dismiss the Bible and God Himself, in order to promote their agenda and control the American people.

Christian Conservative Americans experience occasional victories which can fool us into thinking that we can relax our vigilance. However, just because one issue is won today does not mean we are safe tomorrow. We must remain diligent and steadfast. For instance, Hillary Clinton pushed for a healthcare mandate during her husband's presidency. Luckily "Hillary-care" went down in flames. Freedom loving Americans rejoiced across the nation. Little did we know it would be re-introduced years later, but this time would pass.

CHAPTER 11

SAME SEX MARRIAGE

Victory initially went to the conservatives on the issue of gay marriage. At first gay activists and those who support them did not succeed. So they tried, and they tried again. When they could not get the populace to agree, they found another avenue: the courts. Actually, the courts are the weapons of choice for most of the battle fronts of this war on America. Is it a surprise, when we hear that the Supreme Court Justices are now telling other nations not to adopt constitutions similar to the United States Constitution?

The extreme homosexual agenda has found a foothold in our courts. Even when the populace of a state speaks by vote and says they do not want homosexual marriages allowed in the state, the state courts have ruled that the state must recognize gay marriages.

If our government abided by the first amendment and separated itself from the Church, gay marriage could be legalized by the states or the government could be silent on the issue without any consequence. In other words, gay marriage could be legal, but no church that followed the Bible would perform such marriages. However, I do have a slight problem with this approach due to the fact that there are more and more churches breaking from the Scriptures by following the desires of men rather than the desires of God.

However, this is not my greatest fear in regard to homosexual marriage. As a pastor and a citizen who has seen what the government is doing concerning the Church, my greatest fear is the loss of the first amendment rights that are secured by the Constitution. I can foresee a day when military chaplains will be forced to perform marriages for homosexual couples. I can see the day when pastors and churches will be sued for not providing these marriages.

If the government was silent and churches followed biblical principles, gay marriage would not be an issue. However, our government has an agenda. Gay marriage is one of the issues the current administration not only supports but promotes.

In the book of Genesis the Bible relays God's concern that it was not good that man should be alone. Adam named all the animals that the Lord brought before him, but for Adam there was no help. So, the Lord caused Adam to fall into a deep sleep: and as he slept, the Lord took one of Adam's ribs out and closed up Adam's flesh. Then the Lord took that rib and made a woman and introduced her to Adam. Adam called her woman because she was bone of his bone and flesh of his flesh. Then the Bible says something interesting, "Therefore shall a man leave his father and his mother, and shall cleave unto his wife: and they shall be one flesh." (Genesis 2:18-24)

As Christians, marriage was instituted by God, between one man and one woman. Any deviation from this definition is in error; whether it is gay marriage, bigamy, polygamy, or bestiality.

I find it interesting that those on the left want homosexuals to get married in the first place, since marriage was instituted by God and established in His Word. But then again, the real reason for this item on the left's agenda is not for the union of gay couples to be recognized by God, but to pervert the things of God. This is another attack on our Judeo-Christian values and explains why heterosexuals are discouraged to marry, while homosexuals are trying to marry in droves. Please do not misunderstand; I do not suggest we put homosexuals to death as was the practice during Old Testament times.

> Leviticus 20:13 If a man also lie with mankind, as he lieth with a woman, both of them have committed an abomination: they shall surely be put to death; their blood *shall be* upon them.

However, neither do I suggest that as a society we be forced to recognize and even outwardly support any issue that God Himself does not recognize or support. The New Testament is clear about both effeminacy and homosexuality.

> (1Co 6:9) Know ye not that the unrighteous shall not inherit the kingdom of God? Be not deceived: neither fornicators, nor idolaters, nor adulterers, nor effeminate, nor abusers of themselves with mankind,

It may not be popular in today's world, but nevertheless the Bible is extremely clear about those men who act like women and about homosexuality. Without being too graphic, "abusers of themselves with mankind" is a reference to a homosexual act.

I recognize and appreciate that we do not live in a Theocracy. Therefore, I am not suggesting that we make homosexuality a crime. However, not making it a crime and sanctioning homosexual marriage are two entirely different things. When the government and some church organizations condone a behavior, the behavior will become more widespread.

This explains why Christianity as a whole is less effective than in times past. At one point, Christianity spoke with one voice on the issue of homosexuality. Now America hears a conflicted, bi-polar response from the church on this topic. Those churches that have strayed from Scripture chiefly regarding gay marriage but also in regard to other issues have caused harm to Christianity. But not only have they harmed the Church, they have harmed America and they even have hurt the person who practices homosexuality. By condoning sin, we tell those bound by that sin that either there is no need for forgiveness or that their actions are not sinful. This means the person will have to live in that sin forever and will never be set free. Some churches do not preach the truth about sin because the leaders of these churches do not believe that sin is real.

However, Proverbs says, "Righteousness exalteth a nation: but sin *is* a reproach to any people." If the church in America is silent on sin, America will find itself a reproach. If we long for this great nation to be exalted; we need to be righteous and promote righteousness.

The federal government should be involved in very few aspects of the lives of the citizens. The government's involvement should primarily involve defense: defense of the nation and defense of the Constitution including the right to life, liberty, and the pursuit of happiness.

However, with rights come responsibilities. Though I have not yet mentioned the dual role of rights and responsibilities it is of the utmost importance. You may have the right to pursue happiness, but you have the responsibility to pursue it yourself. In other words, if you have not found happiness, it is not the fault of society or the government. It is your own fault.

Having said that, I fully recognize that government regulations can and do impede the pursuit of happiness, but happiness itself is not derived from the government. Happiness for the Christian comes from God.

Psalm 16:11 Thou wilt shew me the path of life: in thy presence *is* fulness of joy; at thy right hand *there are* pleasures for evermore.

Looking to the government for our happiness is a symptom of our lack of reliance on the Lord. If we need more joy, we need to get back into His presence. There is a war on God in America because the left derives its power from dependence on government. If Americans get back into the presence of God we will realize there is fullness of joy and at His right hand are pleasures for evermore. With God's presence fully realized in America, there would be no need for the government to create happiness and the strangle-hold of the left would be released. However, the left's power would also be reduced, thus the reason for the war with God in America.

Outsourcing

I am amazed at the number of relevant, current issues the Bible discusses. Even when the issues change with the times, the changeless Word continues to address every circumstance which arises. God's Word is timeless. His Word was true the day He inspired men to write it and will remain true until the end of time. Whether our concern is groupthink, taxes, a strong military or any other current topic, it is addressed by the Bible.

When recessions come so come the voices saying too many American jobs are exported to other countries. The answer seems always to be the same: raise taxes. It's not called a tax increase; it is called a tariff. But don't be fooled by the name, tariffs are not paid by the foreign companies. They are added to the price you pay when you buy the product. The same can be said about corporate taxes. When taxes are levied on a company, the company does not pay the tax, ultimately the consumer pays it. The left's dual desires to raise taxes on the rich and keep jobs in America are incompatible. If we want more jobs in this nation, we can have them overnight by lowering taxes.

This seems obvious, but then again we are not politicians. Something that is just common sense to the rest of us is rocket science to the typical politician (especially those on the left). Their answer to preventing jobs from being outsourced is not to reduce the tax burden on American companies, which would insure their continued viability while enticing foreign companies into America. No, that is too easy. Their solution is to increase regulation and raise taxes on businesses, punishing success and discouraging expansion. This was the same approach King Rehoboam took with Israel; it backfired and the nation was divided.

Clearly Rehoboam did not have the wisdom God gave his father, King Solomon. Solomon actually used the outsourcing of labor to the benefit of the kingdom:

> 1Kings 5:6-12 Now therefore command thou that they hew me cedar trees out of Lebanon; and my servants shall be with thy servants: and unto thee will I give hire for thy servants according to all that thou shalt appoint: for thou knowest that *there is* not among us any that can skill to hew timber like unto the Sidonians.7) And it came to pass, when Hiram heard the words of Solomon, that he rejoiced greatly, and said, Blessed *be* the LORD this day, which hath given unto David a wise son over this great people.8) And Hiram sent to Solomon, saying, I have considered the things which thou sentest to me for: *and* I will do all thy desire concerning timber of cedar, and concerning timber of fir.9) My servants shall bring *them* down from Lebanon unto the sea: and I will convey them by sea in floats unto the place that thou shalt appoint me, and will cause them to be discharged there, and thou shalt receive *them:* and thou shalt accomplish my desire, in giving food for my household.10) So Hiram gave Solomon cedar trees and fir trees *according to* all his desire.11) And Solomon gave Hiram twenty thousand measures of wheat *for* food to his household, and twenty

measures of pure oil: thus gave Solomon to Hiram year by year.12) And the LORD gave Solomon wisdom, as he promised him: and there was peace between Hiram and Solomon; and they two made a league together.

Solomon outsourced jobs to Lebanon. This not only benefited Solomon by giving him the product he greatly desired, but it benefited Lebanon by the purchase. And there was another unforeseen benefit of this arrangement. We see in verse 12 that there was a "league" made between these two nations. Peace a by-product of outsourcing.

If we provide jobs or services to others, the trade arrangement becomes a great motivator for us to understand the other party's needs and desires. Our concern becomes how we can best provide for them. Hence, outsourcing encourages peace and agreement.

The real problem the left has with outsourcing jobs is that it promotes competition and capitalism. They claim outsourcing harms the American economy. If liberals had a plan on how the United States could become more competitive and how we could create a more advantageous business environment in comparison to foreign countries, I would love to hear it. Furthermore, I would most likely be in favor of it. However, the main solution offered is more government intervention. Government intervention only interferes with American business practices by limiting competition and reducing efficiency, which in turn limits companies' ability to deliver a better, cheaper product.

To slow the growth of outsourcing, two main tactics have been considered by liberals: (1) boycotting products made by American companies who outsource employment to foreign countries and (2) government interference in the private sector. Boycotting products, though impractical due to the number of people it takes to significantly impact large corporations, is at least a way people can express themselves as private citizens through their own pocketbooks. Government interference is the most feasible avenue, but the disadvantages far outweigh the presumed benefits.

One avenue the government has taken is to increase the length of time unemployment benefits are paid. Unfortunately, there is no such thing as free money. Someone has to pay for the benefits given to people who are not producing. Either more money must be printed, which eventually leads to inflation, or taxes must be raised.

In an inflationary climate, every dollar will buy less because every dollar is worth less. In a highly taxed economy, there are fewer dollars circulating in the private sector, so there are fewer dollars available for consumers to spend to stimulate economic growth. Neither option is very appealing. Inflated prices, as well as decreasing private sector wealth, result in worsening employment prospects. The marketplace just does not have the revenue needed to employ the unemployed. Therefore, government intervention only serves to slow the growth of the economy and impede the production of new employment opportunities.

Thomas Paine (1776) wrote about his anxiety when he penned, "Government, even in its best state, is but a necessary evil; in its worst state, an intolerable one."

The founding fathers understood the danger of government interference in the private sector when they wrote:

> No State shall without the consent of Congress, lay any imposts or duties on imports or exports, except what may be absolutely necessary for executing its inspection laws; and the net produce of all the duties and impost, laid by any state on imports and exports, shall be for the

use of the treasury of the United States; and all such laws shall be subject to the revision and control of Congress." (Congress, 1789, article 1 section 10 clause 2).

In other words, one of the states cannot assess a tax on goods brought in from another state, nor can they prohibit the exportation of jobs to another state. A term commonly used for this is a free market or a capitalistic society.

Free trade between states has elevated America to the pinnacle of financial success in the world. It is not a far stretch to go from an interstate free market to an international free market. An interstate free market with limited government interference has had a tremendous impact on the American economy. Using this principle in the international arena would have a beneficial effect on both the American and the foreign economies.

Profit is the primary reason that companies exist. For a company to make a profit, it must reach a balance between providing quality products and services and managing expenses.

America's wealth and standing in the world are due in part to the ability of the people to compete for profit and the limitations placed on the government to interfere with this process.

The founding fathers foresaw a day when the government would intrude into the affairs of its citizens. "The enumeration in the Constitution of certain rights shall not be construed to deny or disparage others retained by the people." (Congress, 1789, Amendment 9). This is to say that the specific rights listed in the Constitution cannot be interpreted to imply that we, the people, have no other rights than those listed. Therefore, citizens have rights not addressed by the Constitution.

The rights guaranteed to citizens, though not completely extendable to businesses, do somewhat encompass them because businesses are owned and run by people. When government interferes with a business, it interferes with the people. When government interferes with the people, it interferes with you and me. This is yet another reason to maintain the limits placed on government by the Constitution.

Retaining and enforcing Constitutional limits on the government will create economic prosperity. The growth of the businesses which can outsource employment without government interference translates into quality products available at a cheaper price and results in an increasing number of jobs in America. However, the true solution to decreasing the number of American jobs which are outsourced to foreign countries is to reduce regulations on businesses and to lower the taxes they are forced to pay. 7

CHAPTER 12

CONCLUSION

Honestly, there are too many critical issues and too many eradicated liberties to address in this one book. As I write, there are more laws being passed, more regulations being imposed, and more freedoms being stifled. Therefore, instead of trying to address every new intrusion on our liberties in the conclusion of this book, I will let Paul speak about his beliefs on the topic of liberty.

In 2 Corinthians Paul writes about liberty and the law when he says, "Ye are our epistle written in our hearts, known and read of all men." He continues, "ye are manifestly declared to be the epistle of Christ . . . written not with ink, but with the Spirit of the living God; not in tables of stone, but in fleshy tables of the heart." In other words, the things Christians do are done, because God has moved our hearts, not because He has forced us to obey a set of laws. Paul writes, "Such trust have we through Christ to God-ward: Not that we are sufficient of ourselves to think anything as of ourselves; but our sufficiency is of God." Basically, Paul means that we can put our trust in God through Christ Jesus, not because there is anything great about us, but because there is everything GREAT about God. We could not accomplish anything on our own, but through Him we are more than conquerors. Paul reminds the Corinthians that God, "also hath made us able ministers of the New Testament; not of the letter, but of the spirit: for the letter killeth, but the spirit giveth life." According to Paul, "the letter", also known as the law kills; however, the Spirit gives life. In America, we need fewer laws and more of His Spirit. If we had more of His Spirit, we would not need many of our current laws. America is in need of a modern-day Great Awakening. I pray I will be used in even a small way in America's coming great revival.

Paul discusses the difference between the Old and New Testaments. He refers to the Old Testament as the "ministration of death." He says that it was written and engraved on stone, and though it was glorious for the time, the New Testament's "ministration of the Spirit" exceeds the law in glory. In other words, the Law of Moses was a gift to God's people when it was needed, but Christ brought a better law. The new law is not one written on stones, but written on our hearts. When the Law was written in stone, man could go in the darkness of night and in the shadows he could indulge in sin, however, when the law is written on our hearts, it is impossible to escape. God continues to tug and pull until sin is relinquished. Paul wrote about the freedom we have in Jesus: "Now the Lord is that Spirit: and where the Spirit of the Lord is, there is liberty." Paul has given us one of the best reasons to pursue a renewal of the Spirit of God in America. Wherever His Spirit is there is liberty. (Paraphrased from 2 Corinthians 3:2-18)

Where the Spirit of the Lord resides, there is the right to life, the right to liberty, and the right to pursue happiness.

The liberation brought by God's presence in the hearts of His people is detrimental to the agenda of those on the left. Progressives must, therefore change the context of the discussion.

Those of the progressive movement tell us that there are no absolutes. As Bible-believing Christians, we are a threat to the proliferation of the message of the left because God and His Word are very clear. If we hold to God's unchanging truths, we realize the Bible does not change in order to fit into our climate. Instead God's Word explains that God expects us to change to fit into His parameters. Similarly, the Constitution and Declaration of Independence, which I believe were divinely inspired, are not to change to fit into the ideology professed by a particular administration, but those who govern must change their actions to fit into the parameters of the Constitution and founding documents. This principle alone gives great insight into the perceived danger posed by Christianity to those on the left in America. Like the Bible, the United States Constitution is clear. The Bible and the Constitution are still black and white even when they are abandoned, when they are twisted, and when they are unread.

Unfortunately, the Bible, the Constitution, and the Declaration of Independence have for the most part been unread by the majority of the American people. The lack of knowledge about these documents explains why misquotes from the Bible and from our founding documents lead people to believe untruths about what both documents say and what they do not say. If the general public read the Bible and the founding documents, the progressives' ability to alter the meanings of words in public discourse would be squelched. As it is, though, the left is able to use people's lack of knowledge, group think, and political correctness to change the arguments. Those who stand against their agenda are ridiculed.

Progressives have recently turned things upside down in government and politics. We are told that all good things come from government, that there is a proper order in which these things should flow. Their mantra is that power begins in Washington, and flows to the state capitol and then, to the county and local governments. The progressive ideal for the order in which power should flow is the opposite of what was designed by the founders of this great nation.

Furthermore, the progressive belief in the origination of power in the government, flowing to the people is contrary to true liberty. Liberty does not come from the government but from God. Power does not come from some centralized locale, but from the people. The proper flow of power in keeping with our liberties would be that God empowers the individual and the individual empowers the county and local governments. A combination of the individual and the county and local governments empower the state governments which then empower the federal government. In other words, the federal government is the servant of the state government. The state government is the servant of the county and local governments. The county and local governments are the servants of the individual and the individual is the servant of God.

America is unique in that our founders believed in a national sovereignty that began with God as the endower of all rights, and the individual. The individual, in turn, entrusts some authority to government. The sovereignty of the individual is not endowed by government which grants individual power based on their social position or class. The latter method would leave powerless those individuals whom the government found unworthy based on race, religion, sex, or any other attribute that those in power chose. However, because sovereignty begins with the individual and flows upwards from there, all are to be treated equally under the law.

Our founders' core belief in the individual sovereignty, which they recorded in the founding documents, as well as in their auxiliary writings, lead to freedom for slaves and women's suffrage, among other things. A breach in the sovereignty of any American is an affront to the sovereignty of all.

In the Gospel of Matthew, Jesus was approached by a Roman Centurion who had a servant lying sick at home from palsy. Jesus told the Centurion that He would go to his home and perform a miracle. The Centurion responded, "Lord, I am not worthy that thou shouldest come under my roof: but speak the word only, and my servant shall be healed." His next words are very insightful. "For I am a man **under authority**, having soldiers under me: and I say to this man, Go, and he goeth; and to another, come, and he cometh; and to my servant, Do this, and he doeth it." Jesus was amazed by the man's understanding and declared that He had not seen such faith in all of Israel. (Matthew 8:5-10)

This Centurion's wisdom is revealed upon closer examination. By remarking that he was a man under authority, he revealed his understanding of the fact that as a public official, he was a servant of the people. This concept is lost by many people in places of authority today. It has been lost by many pastors, ministers, politicians, police officers, teachers, and judges. Those entrusted by the people to leadership positions should not be viewed as being in a "higher" position than others, but as people who are humbled beneath the responsibility of authority. If you are under authority, you are to serve those who are in your care. You are to be their servant.

In Germany during the trials of some of the Nazis leaders who ruled with Hitler, the excuse was given that they were only enforcing the law as part of their job. Thankfully, they were still found guilty and sentenced to death. Today, we hear those exact same words echoed by those in authority here in America.

When we are told to empty our pockets, take off our shoes, remove our belts, and then are forced to watch as our children are touched by strangers before boarding an airplane, we are told that they are only doing their job. When the police set up check points and stop us without just cause while we are trying to get to our destination, we are told that they are only doing their job.

If your job requires you to abandon the Constitution and the Declaration of Independence, if your job asks you to violate the rights of another individual, you will be held accountable by God, if not by men. If this describes you and your job, be a better American, and quit. Find a job that does more than swears to uphold the Constitution then forsakes it; find a career that honors every American and his or her God-given rights.

As government continues to expand into more and more of our lives, I dream of the possibility that one day there will be a law requiring every bill that is brought before Congress to reference the part of the Constitution that permits the new law. I would even be happy if each new law passed automatically included a sunset requirement.

Wouldn't it be great if most laws passed by Congress were required to be reconsidered every few years? Why does it seem that sunset clauses are only attached to tax cuts? Why do tax hikes never have an expiration date? The answer is painfully obvious to me; the government has an insatiable appetite for our money. When tax cuts are proposed, politicians act like they are being forced to go on a diet. Continuing with this metaphor, a sunset clause makes the diet more palatable by showing them when they will be allowed to eat what they want again. The government not only wants off the diet, but wants more food than is in the fridge.

Just think of the possibilities of a sunset requirement for every new law! Not only would the laws expire, but the politicians would have to defend the law every time they came up for another vote. The sunset requirement would insure that there would be no difference between the politics practiced in election years versus non-election year politics in Washington, D.C. Congressmen would have to support or rescind "sunsetting" laws passed every year. If Congress votes to take more of our liberties away with new laws or does not rescind old liberty-infringing laws the voters would be more likely to remember and remove the offending politicians from office. Examples of laws that reduce our liberties and which should be reconsidered often concern healthcare, seatbelts, light bulbs, and other regulations which restrict the rights of the people who are doing no harm to their neighbors.

When will the American people decide we have had enough? When will we speak with one loud voice and say, "Give me back my liberty, give me back my freedom!"? We were told that we needed to give up some of our freedom because of the war on terror; however, now we are told that the war on terror is over or at least coming to an end and there is no talk of giving back the liberties that were stolen. How right was Benjamin Franklin when he said, "Those who would give up essential liberty to purchase a little temporary safety deserve neither liberty nor safety."!

I struggled in my heart and mind about whether to write this book and to seek to have it published. Being a pastor, I heard and had listened to those people around me who said politics does not belong in the Church. Many believe pastors have no business speaking out about politics from the pulpit. However, as I began to look around, I realized there were almost no pastors speaking up for true Christian American principles, the Judeo-Christian values upon which our country was founded. Pastors who have spoken up have been demonized by the left, and their allies in the mainstream media, for the purpose of creating fear in the remainder of us, thus keeping us quiet.

As I considered the fear that was dwelling inside me, I was forced to ask myself a question. If I don't speak up, who will? If not now, when? If YOU don't speak up, who will? If not now, when? It was Edmund Burke who said, "All that is necessary for evil to triumph is for good men to do nothing." Well, it is time for good, decent men and women across this nation to stand against the onslaught of propaganda being fed to our next generation; it is time for us as Christian Americans to do something.

I believe this nation is still full of good, God-fearing men and women who, when they realize the challenges of the day, will rise to the cause of liberty. Alexis de Tocqueville said, "America is great because she is good. If America ceases to be good, America will cease to be great." For the record, I still believe most Americans hold dear the values that made this nation great.

It is time for us to shake off the new taskmaster called government and return to the liberty and freedom that God outlined in His Word and promised our forefathers.